Countries OF THE WORLD

Colombia

Gareth Stevens Publishing
A WORLD ALMANAC EDUCATION GROUP COMPANY

About the Author: Dr. Leslie Jermyn is a professional anthropologist who has done field research in both South and Central America. She has written largely for academic audiences but draws on her extensive teaching experience to inform her popular writing.

Written by
LESLIE JERMYN

Edited by
LEELA VENGADASALAM

Designed by
LYNN CHIN

Picture research by
THOMAS KHOO

Updated and reprinted in 2005.
First published in North America in 1999 by
Gareth Stevens Publishing
A World Almanac Education Group Company
330 West Olive Street, Suite 100
Milwaukee, Wisconsin 53212 USA

Please visit our web site at
www.garethstevens.com
For a free color catalog describing
Gareth Stevens Publishing's
list of high-quality books
and multimedia programs,
call 1-800-542-2595 (USA)
or 1-800-387-3178 (Canada).
Gareth Stevens Publishing's fax:
(414) 332-3567.

© **TIMES EDITIONS PTE LTD 1999**
© **TIMES MEDIA PRIVATE LIMITED 2000**
© **MARSHALL CAVENDISH INT'L (ASIA) PRIVATE LIMITED 2005**
Originated and designed by Times Editions–Marshall Cavendish
An imprint of Marshall Cavendish International (Asia) Private Limited
A member of Times Publishing Limited
Times Centre, 1 New Industrial Road
Singapore 536196
http://www.marshallcavendish.com/genref

Library of Congress Cataloging-in-Publication Data
Jermyn, Leslie
Colombia / by Leslie Jermyn.
p. cm. -- (Countries of the world)
Includes bibliographical references (p. 94) and index.
Summary: An overview of the South American nation of Colombia
that includes information on its geography, history, government,
lifestyles, language, customs, and current issues.
ISBN 0-8368-2308-7 (lib. bdg.)
1. Colombia -- Juvenile literature. [1. Colombia.] I.Title.
II. Series: Countries of the world (Milwaukee, Wis.)
F2258.5.J47   1999
986.1 -- dc21   99-11354

Printed in Singapore

5 6 7 8 9 07 06 05

PICTURE CREDITS
Archive Photos: 35, 36, 69 (right), 70, 76, 84
BES Stock: cover
Camera Press Ltd.: 48, 58, 59, 60, 78
Victor Englebert: 7, 8, 9 (top), 11 (top), 17,
    19, 23 (bottom), 25, 26, 27, 28, 30, 31,
    34, 37, 42, 53, 55, 56, 61, 63, 64, 67, 68,
    77, 80, 81, 83, 87, 91
Eduardo Gil: 3 (center), 18, 23 (top), 40, 47,
    62, 72, 73,
HBL Network Photo Agency: 79
The Hutchison Library: 3 (top), 5, 6,
    9 (bottom), 16, 20, 21 (both), 32 (top),
    33, 38, 41, 43, 49, 50, 51 (both), 52,
    57 (both), 69 (left), 85
Klingwall: 12 (bottom), 54, 65
Rodolfo Llinás: 82 (right)
North Wind Picture Archives: 12 (top), 74
Adriana C. Ocampo: 82 (left)
Chip and Rosa Maria Peterson: 1, 2, 4,
    10, 11 (bottom), 13, 15 (both), 22, 24,
    32 (bottom), 45, 46, 71
South American Pictures: 3 (bottom), 29, 39
Lesley Thelander: 14
Topham Picturepoint: 44, 66, 75, 89

Digital Scanning by Superskill Graphics Pte Ltd

Contents

AN OVERVIEW OF COLOMBIA

The fourth largest country in South America, Colombia bears the name of the discoverer of the Americas, Christopher Columbus. For a country seven times smaller than Brazil, its geography, including the flora and fauna, is one of the most diverse in South America. Just as varied are Colombia's warm and friendly inhabitants. The population includes a small percentage of native Indian groups, some of whom have maintained their traditional lifestyles. There are about four hundred Indian tribes in the country now. Although Colombia's history has been a violent one with wars and guerilla activity, the economy is stable. In fact, it has one of the highest rates of economic growth of any South American country.

Opposite: Cycling, like soccer, is an imported spectator sport that has become popular in Colombia. A cycling race in the country draws many participants as well as spectators.

Below: Old-style Colombian buses, or *chivas* (CHEE-vahs), travel the roads in the countryside. The body of the bus is made of painted wood.

THE FLAG OF COLOMBIA

The Colombian flag is similar to the flags of Ecuador and Venezuela. These countries, together with Panama, were once under Spanish control and were known as New Granada. In 1819, this territory gained independence and was renamed Gran Colombia. The colors of the flag are those adopted by Francisco de Miranda, a Venezuelan freedom fighter. The colors symbolize that the nation (yellow) was separated from Spain by the sea (blue). The red symbolizes the liberation of the South American territories and the blood shed by those who fought in wars for independence. The current form of the flag was adopted in 1861.

Geography

The Land

Colombia is located in the northwestern corner of South America, where the continent joins the Isthmus of Panama. It covers an area of 440,831 square miles (1,141,752 square kilometers). Its population of more than 42 million people is the third largest in Latin America. The capital is Santa Fé de Bogotá.

Colombia has coastlines on both the Pacific Ocean and the Caribbean Sea, and it borders five countries: Panama, Venezuela, Brazil, Peru, and Ecuador. Some islands in the Pacific and the Caribbean are part of Colombian territory, too. For instance, in the Pacific, 270 miles (434 km) west of Buenaventura, lies the Colombian-controlled island of Malpelo. A collection of two islands — San Andrés and Providencia — and thirteen cays off the coast of Nicaragua also belong to Colombia. There are other islands in this area claimed by Colombia, but the claim is disputed by Nicaragua.

In terms of topography, Colombia can be divided into four distinct regions: the Andean highlands, the Caribbean lowlands, the Pacific lowlands, and the Eastern plains. These regions are separated mostly by one or more of the three parallel mountain ranges, or cordilleras, of the Andes Mountains. These cordilleras are known as the Cordillera Occidental (western), Cordillera Central, and Cordillera Oriental (eastern).

PIRATES AND PATOIS: SAN ANDRÉS AND PROVIDENCIA

Colonized by the English in 1631, the islands of San Andrés and Providencia came under Spanish control in 1786. Colombia took control of them in 1822. One interesting detail about the history of these islands is the legend of the treasure on San Andrés, which has still not been found. *(A Closer Look, page 70)*

Below: Sierra Nevada de Santa Marta in northern Colombia has snowcapped mountains, including the highest peak in Colombia, Cristóbal Colón at 18,947 feet (5,775 meters).

Above: **Colombian women wash clothes by the Atrato River. Called Río Atrato in Spanish, the river, which is 416 miles (670 km) long, flows north to the Gulf of Urabá on the Caribbean.**

The Andean highlands are bordered on the east and west by the outlying cordilleras. Between these great mountain chains lie fertile river valleys, such as the Cauca and the Magdalena, home to about 40 percent of the population. Bogotá is located in a basin within the Cordillera Oriental. Running between the Cordillera Central and the Cordillera Oriental, before draining into the Caribbean Sea, is the Magdalena River, the most important river in the country.

The Caribbean lowlands are in northern Colombia, along the Caribbean Sea. The three most important ports of Cartagena, Barranquilla, and Santa Marta are on this coast. Inland from the coast are areas where crops are cultivated. To the north is Sierra Nevada de Santa Marta, which has the highest mountain peaks in the country.

The Pacific lowlands include the small strip of coastline between the ocean and the Cordillera Occidental. The only significant urban center in this region is the port of Buenaventura.

Eastern Colombia is the largely flat area bordering Venezuela and Brazil. This area includes part of the Amazon and Orinoco river basins. Although this region is about 60 percent of the country's territory, only 2 percent of the population lives there.

THE MAGDALENA: COLOMBIA'S WATERY HIGHWAY

Known as "the lifeline of Colombia," the Magdalena River has been an important route for transporting goods on keelboats since the Spanish conquered the country. This river also supports a large freshwater fishing industry.

(A Closer Look, page 64)

Climate

There is little seasonal variation in temperature in Colombia because it is close to the equator. It is an area where the climate of different regions is determined by altitude — the higher you are above sea level, the colder it is. With three distinct chains of mountains, Colombia has many different altitude zones. Coastal lowland areas are known as "hot country" and have annual mean temperatures of 75° Fahrenheit (24° Centigrade). "Temperate country" includes most of the settled valleys and basins in the Andean region between altitudes of 304 feet (93 m) and 912 feet (278 m). Temperatures in these areas range from 55° F (13° C) to 65° (18° C). "Cold country" is above 912 feet (278 m), and, there, temperatures are 55° F (13° C) or lower, depending on altitude. The only seasonal change is between wet and dry seasons, which alternate about every three months. La Guajira Peninsula, located at the northern tip of the country, is the driest place in Colombia, with an average annual rainfall of only 10 inches (254 millimeters). In contrast, cities in Chocó department, or state, near the Pacific Ocean have an average annual rainfall of 400 inches (10,150 mm).

Above: **A rain forest in Nariño, southwestern Colombia, receives good annual rainfall.**

Plants

Colombia covers less than 1 percent of Earth's surface, but it contains about 15 percent of all known living species. The range of ecosystems, from high mountains to tropical coasts and river plains, means plants requiring almost any type of rainfall and soil conditions have found a home in Colombia. There are 55,000 species of plants, of which 20,000 are endemic, meaning they are found only in Colombia.

Animals and Birds

Colombia has 358 species of mammals, including wild cats, such as jaguars and *tigrillo* (tee-GREE-yoh), and colored and spectacled bears, so named because of the dark patches around their eyes. Fifteen percent of all living primates (the order that contains humans) live here. Of the 8,000 known species of birds, 1,700 are found in Colombia. They include mountain birds, such as eagles; jungle birds, such as colorful quetzals, parrots, macaws, hummingbirds, and toucans; and pelagic birds, such as petrels, frigate birds, and gulls, which live on small islands far out to sea.

Above: **A scarlet macaw makes a pretty picture on the branch of an Amazon rain forest tree.**

Left: **Yellow highland flowers add color to the Colombian landscape.**

NATURE'S MAGICIANS: BUTTERFLIES

Every ecosystem has its share of insects, and, perhaps, the most beautiful are butterflies. Colombia has over three thousand species of them.
(A Closer Look, page 66)

History

The Early Years

Colombia was named after the famous explorer Christopher Columbus, although he never actually visited the country. When the Spaniards first arrived in 1499, the area that later became Colombia was occupied by indigenous peoples. The biggest of the pre-Columbian tribes was the Chibcha, who lived in the highlands and were ruled by a chief called Bacatá. They used coins made of gold and carved beautiful jewelry from that precious metal. Shortly after the Spanish conquest, however, their numbers were reduced by about 90 percent.

Although a pilot of Columbus's fleet touched the coast of Colombia in 1499, the first port at Santa Marta was not established until 1525. In 1536, Gonzalo Jiménez de Quesada headed an expedition inland. He led a party of 670 Spaniards up the Magdalena River. Eleven months after they set out, they reached the Eastern Cordillera, at a place near modern-day Vélez, with only 200 survivors. Close to what is now Bogotá, they encountered the Chibchas, who challenged the newcomers to a battle. The Spaniards won because they were on horseback. The remaining Indians scattered. Because they had never seen horses before, they believed the Spaniards had magical powers.

Quesada's claim over this region did not go unchallenged. Two other Spanish expeditions arrived there at around the same time. The first of these to arrive was a force from Peru, and the second was a group from the plains of Venezuela. All three expeditions wanted gold and to claim the area for themselves. The question of ownership was not settled for fourteen years. In the end, King Charles of Spain decided that Quesada had the rightful claim to the lands.

In 1538, Santa Fé de Bogotá was founded, and, by 1549, it had become the administrative center for the territory of New Granada. In 1718, New Granada separated completely from the Viceroyalty of Peru. It included the territories of what are now Colombia, Panama, Ecuador, and Venezuela.

By the end of the 1700s, people of European descent born in the New World began to resent the power and control exercised by those from Spain. New ideas about independence began to

Above: **A replica of Columbus's Santa María caravel, or sailing vessel, can be seen at the Museo Nacional in Bogotá.**

SAN AGUSTÍN: A 3,000-YEAR-OLD MYSTERY

San Agustín is a small village near the Ecuador border. It is famous for its stone sculptures, which were carved by a mysterious civilization. Today, San Agustín is one of the most important archaeological sites in South America.

(A Closer Look, page 72)

Left: **The Monument to Independence stands on the site where Simón Bolívar and his comrades won their battle against the Spaniards in 1819.**

circulate, and, soon, leaders for the cause of independence emerged. Simón Bolívar led the fight in New Granada. In 1810, Bolívar organized resistance to the Spanish crown in Venezuela and Colombia. His dream was to see the entire Spanish-speaking area of South America united under one flag. Most other leaders, however, wanted autonomy for their areas and did not cooperate with Bolívar.

This lack of cooperation gave the Spanish crown another chance to control the rebel colonies. In 1815, to reestablish colonial control, Spain sent a force of 11,000 soldiers under the command of General Pablo Morillo. For two years, Morillo swept through Colombia, murdering and butchering everyone he thought had supported independence. Morillo only served to convince people they had to get rid of the Spaniards.

Independence

Bolívar had gone into exile when Morillo arrived, but he returned in 1818. For the next three years, Bolívar and his Colombian-born ally Francisco de Paula Santander fought the Spaniards, taking back one city after another until all of modern-day Colombia was free of Spanish control. By 1826, all the former colonies of Spain in South America had achieved full independence.

Below: **In 1815, General Pablo Morillo reestablished Spanish control over Colombia.**

Post-Independence

Bolívar created the first constitution of the country in 1821, establishing Gran Colombia, which included Colombia, Ecuador, Venezuela, and what later became Panama. Bolívar left Santander in charge of the new nation and went south to fight for the independence of Ecuador, Peru, and Bolivia. By the time he returned in 1827, the union was in disarray. Bolívar ruled as a dictator for two years and died in 1830. His death marked the end of the Gran Colombia experiment, and since then, Colombia, Ecuador, and Venezuela have been separate countries.

The division between those who supported Bolívar's idea of a strong central government and those who supported Santander's idea of federalism, or weak central government, continued in the new nation in the form of two main political parties: the conservatives and the liberals. Although their methods differed, the parties had somewhat similar goals, and people tended to support whichever party their parents supported. The first hundred years of Colombian nationhood saw many major and minor civil wars, wars with Ecuador, overthrow of governments, and five different constitutions. The last constitution, written in 1886, was in effect until 1991.

Above: Simón Bolívar, also called *El Libertador,* or the Liberator, led the revolution that defeated the Spaniards in Colombia. He was responsible for overthrowing Spanish rule in much of South America.

Left: **Gustavo Rojas Pinilla took control of the government in 1953, when Colombia experienced some of the worst violence in its modern history.**

The Twentieth Century

At the start of the twentieth century, Colombia was in the throes of a bloody civil war — the War of a Thousand Days. It began in 1899, when the liberals tried to unseat a conservative president. By the time the war ended in 1903, approximately one hundred thousand Colombians had died, leaving Colombia weak and opening the door to U.S. intervention. After helping Panama gain independence from Colombia, the United States encouraged American companies to operate in Colombia. By the 1920s, Colombia was borrowing heavily from the United States and was forced to accept American control of Panama.

Violence continued to plague Colombia. The period from 1948 to 1958 is known as *La Violencia* (lah vee-oh-LAYN-see-ah), or The Violence. It began with the assassination of Jorge Eliécer Gaitán, a presidential candidate. In 1953, when Gustavo Rojas Pinilla, the commander of the army, took over the government, the violence abated, and some of the guerrilla groups laid down their weapons. When the army began to suppress members of both political parties, however, the violence resumed.

Opposite: **The Plaza de Bolívar in Bogotá, the first public monument in the city, has a statue of Simón Bolívar in the center.**

Fighting and Drug Wars

To end the dictatorship, leaders of the two parties decided to cooperate. They agreed to share control of the government at all levels to avoid violent competition. This coalition, known as the National Front, lasted from 1958 to 1974. The violence between party members eventually subsided, but other forms of violence, especially in the countryside, persisted well into the 1960s.

After 1974, elections were held again, but groups that opposed the traditional political parties and their leaders continued to be repressed. Many rural people organized themselves into guerrilla groups to fight against inequality and the elites. Meanwhile, drug cartels began financing their own paramilitary death squads to kill those opposing their power. By 1988, the violence in the country became known as the Drug Wars, because the drug mafia assassinated and kidnapped government officials to achieve their aims. The combination of guerrilla groups and drug-related terrorism shrouded Colombia in violence, which escalated in the early 1990s. Recent governments have attempted to control the situation by capturing the most powerful drug barons and negotiating with guerrilla groups, and there has been some improvement.

Below: La Violencia **(1948 to 1958) was a black mark on Colombian history. Street battles and guerrilla warfare in the countryside between supporters of the two main political parties devastated the country.**

Gonzalo Jiménez de Quesada (1495–1579)

Born in Spain, Jiménez was a lawyer and quite wealthy until a lawsuit ruined his family. He decided to try his luck in the New World and emigrated with a group led by the governor of the colony of Santa Marta. In 1536, Jiménez was given command of an expedition into the interior. Although he claimed gold and emeralds from the Chibcha Indians and named the area New Granada, he was nearly imprisoned, when he returned to Spain, for treating the native people badly. He left Spain and returned again only in 1545. In old age, Jiménez organized a disastrous expedition to the llanos, the plains that stretch from the Cordillera Central to the border of Venezuela. He died of leprosy in the Cordillera Central.

Gonzalo Jiménez de Quesada

Francisco de Paula Santander (1792–1840)

Santander was more than Bolívar's right-hand man during the fight for freedom from Spain. Santander was born in Cúcuta, near the border between Colombia and Venezuela. At the age of thirteen, he went to Bogotá to study law. He did not finish his studies, because, once the movement for independence began, he supported the cause of the rebels. In 1819, Bolívar gave him command of the rebels in the decisive battle of Boyacá. In 1821, Santander became vice-president of Gran Colombia and served until the union was dissolved in 1830. Three years later, he became the first elected president of New Granada. Today, Santander is revered as a man committed to a constitutional government.

Francisco de Paula Santander

Jorge Eliécer Gaitán (1902–1948)

Gaitán is remembered as Colombia's first modern politician. Despite his humble beginnings, Gaitán worked tirelessly to become a prominent member of the Liberal Party. He was assassinated in 1948, two years before he was expected to win the presidential election. His death caused such huge riots in Bogotá that the event came to be known as the *Bogotazo* (boh-goh-TAH-zoh), or "the strike of Bogotá." Although Gaitán never served as president, he is an important figure in Colombian history. He was one of the first politicians to speak to common people and rely on their support for success.

Government and the Economy

Starting in the late 1980s, there was growing dissatisfaction with the constitution of 1886, which gave political power mostly to the president and very little to Congress and the judiciary. In 1988, Congress made its first attempt at serious constitutional reform, but the effort was soon abandoned. Colombian university students made the government take up the reform issue, and, in the congressional elections of March 1990, they encouraged voters to deposit an extra vote for reform. More than a million extra votes were cast. The Supreme Court ruled the votes a legal means of forcing a change in the constitution. The presidential election of May 1990 included a referendum. Colombians were asked whether they wanted a special assembly to consider a new constitution. The vote was an overwhelming "yes." In December of that year, another election took place to select members for the special assembly. By July 4, 1991, a new constitution was in place.

Opposite: Elections are keenly contested in Colombia. To be eligible to vote, a person must be twenty-one years old and a resident of the appropriate administrative unit (nation, department, or municipality). Universal male suffrage was granted in the 1930s, but women did not gain the right to vote until 1954.

Below: Guards are on round-the-clock duty at the Government Palace in Bogotá.

Legislative power is controlled by Congress, which has two houses: the Senate and the Chamber of Deputies. Members of the Chamber of Deputies are elected by each department. A department is automatically given two deputies, plus one deputy for each 100,000 people living there. The Senate, with 102 members, is elected nationally, except for two seats reserved for indigenous peoples. Under the new constitution, members of Congress can be dismissed by their colleagues or recalled by the voters if they fail to perform their duties.

A third branch of national government is the judiciary. The Supreme Court controls national justice. There is also a special constitutional court, which ensures that the new constitution is obeyed at all levels of government. There are sixty-one judicial districts. Below the level of national government, there are departmental and municipal levels of government. Each of the thirty-two departments has an elected governor. The governor presides over an elected departmental assembly. The municipal level has mayors elected for two-year terms, as well as elected municipal councils.

PRINCIPAL PARTIES

The main political parties in Colombia are the Liberal Party and the Social Conservative Party. Throughout Colombia's history, these two parties have been the only ones with enough support to control the presidency. Recently, the efforts of some independent political movements to become political parties have failed because of poor support from the people.

Economy

Colombia's main trading partner is the United States. Colombia also trades with the other members of the Andean Community of Nations (Bolivia, Ecuador, Peru, and Venezuela), members of the European Union, and Japan. The country's principal imports include transportation equipment, chemicals, metals, paper products, fuels, and electricity. Principal exports include petroleum, rice, tobacco, coffee, bananas, cut flowers, cotton, coal, textiles, and paper. In addition to these products, many others are produced in various sectors of the economy for both export and domestic consumption.

Agriculture and Forestry

Colombia is blessed with many natural resources. It has an ideal climate for growing coffee beans, from which the favorite drink of many people around the world is made. Almost one-sixth of the country's arable land is used to grow coffee plants. Colombia also produces a wide variety of food crops, such as bananas (grown along the Caribbean coast) and potatoes.

Forests cover about half the country. Important forest products are lumber and paper products. About 30 percent of the labor force is employed in agriculture and forestry.

Above: **Exporting freshly cut flowers, such as roses and carnations, makes an important contribution to the Colombian economy.**

Mining and Energy Production

Very few Colombians are employed in mining and energy production, but these sectors make up 40 percent of foreign trade. Colombia produces enough oil for its own needs and has a surplus for export. Not too long ago, new reserves were discovered in the Casanare region of north-central Colombia. This discovery has strengthened the economy since the mid 1990s. Having many rivers, Colombia uses hydroelectric power for about 75 percent of its electricity needs. Colombia also has a particularly good grade of coal. Other mined commodities include silver, iron ore, zinc, copper, and limestone. About 90

EMERALDS: COLOMBIA'S GREEN TREASURE

Colombia is known for its brilliant emeralds. Some people believe these gems possess magical powers. The best ones are available from shops in Bogotá.
(A Closer Look, page 58)

percent of the world's emeralds are mined in Colombia. There are good reserves of gold and platinum as well.

Colombia produces many manufactured goods for domestic consumption. The country's biggest industries turn out food products, beverages, chemicals, and textiles. About 15 percent of the workforce is employed in the manufacturing sector. The majority of the labor force, however, works in the service sector. Although affected by the violence of the drug trade and guerrilla movements, tourism still represents a portion of the Colombian economy.

Above: Miners receive ore by cable. Then the ore is pulverized, or turned into powder. Many miners now have more sophisticated equipment to speed up their work.

People and Lifestyle

Colombia is an incredibly diverse country. Not only are there wide geographic distinctions, but also significant social differences between the various groups of people living in the country. Despite their many differences, however, Colombians' attitudes toward religion and family are fairly uniform.

Living Together in Diversity

The major distinction among Colombians is economic class. There are groups of people who are very poor, groups of people who are very rich, and those who are somewhere in between. Over the past forty years, there has been a decrease in the percentage of the less fortunate in the country. Nevertheless, on average, about half of all Colombian households are considered poor, earning less than U.S. $900 a year. With such a low total income, a family spends half or more of its income on food. At the other end of the spectrum is a group of people who are very rich because they control the land and most businesses. There is also a small group in the middle, people who hold professional jobs and earn enough to live a fairly comfortable life.

THE PAEZ INDIANS

Estimated to number some sixty thousand, Paez Indians live in the southern highlands of Colombia. Although Paez males used to have many wives, the Roman Catholic faith has enforced monogamy. Another change that has had a more serious impact on the Paez is the loss of their land.
(A Closer Look, page 68)

Below: **Guambiano Indians, considered one of the most traditional Indian groups in Colombia, hail from Silvia, a small town 37 miles (60 km) from Popayán.**

20

Left and *below:* Among the different faces of Colombia, mestizos represent about 58 percent of the population, whites about 20 percent, mulattoes about 14 percent, and Afro-Colombians about 7 percent. Indians make up only 1 percent of the population.

Ethnic Groups

Colombians belong to many different ethnic groups. Criollos are of mixed white and mestizo parentage and make up about 80 percent of the population. Other ethnic groups include mestizos (of Indian and white descent); whites (of Spanish descent); mulattoes (of white and black descent); Afro-Colombians (of African descent); and Indians.

Economic background tends to be defined along ethnic lines. Whites, the middle income group, are generally better educated and trained than the rest. People who are a mixture of two or more ethnic groups, such as the criollos and mestizos, straddle the division between rich and poor. The match between ethnic group and economic class has its roots in Colombian history, where Afro-Colombians and Indians were employed as laborers on farms and in businesses owned by the Spaniards, from whom white Colombians descended. Some Afro-Colombians and Indians, through education or talent, have broken out of the laborer stereotype.

There is also a distinction between city dwellers and rural Colombians. Since 1930, there has been a strong trend in Colombia toward urbanization. More and more people have left the countryside for the cities in search of employment and a better life. This trend has slowed in recent years, but Colombia still has about two-thirds of its population living in cities.

AFRO-COLOMBIANS: THE THIRD BRANCH

Black Colombians live on the Caribbean coast, which was once the center of the slave trade; the Pacific coast; and in the Cali region. The greatest concentration of Afro-Colombians is in the Chocó department.

(A Closer Look, page 44)

Above: **This family is enjoying a day at the park.**

Family Life

As in many countries of the world, Colombian family structure and values have undergone change in the past twenty years. Traditionally, the father was head of the household and the main breadwinner. Women stayed at home to care for the children and look after the house. The head of the family felt responsible for the honor of the family name, which meant that women and girls were not allowed too much freedom outside the home. Women, in particular, were not expected to work or be involved in activities beyond the family and church. This traditional family structure was prevalent among middle- and upper middle-class urban families. Poorer families, on the other hand, depended on women's work around the farm or in a job to help supplement the family income. These days, many women of all classes, armed with higher educational qualifications, are joining the workforce.

Among poorer people, urbanization often results in divided families, with some family members going to the city to work. Often, women are left alone with their children without much, or any, financial support from the men in the cities. Despite all the changes and upheavals in recent years, family ties remain strong. Colombian children, for instance, are very close to their parents throughout their lives. They will usually remain at home until they get married, and if they do not have enough money for a place of their own, they might continue to live, with their husbands or wives, in the home of one of their parents.

Godparenting, Colombian-style

Colombians use their family connections to find work or a place to stay or to make important business contacts. There is a special social institution that enables even nonblood relatives to become part of a family unit. This practice is called *compadrazgo* (kohm-pah-DRAHZ-goh) and is similar to godparenting. When a child is born, the parents choose two people from among their friends or associates to be *compadres* (kohm-PAH-drays), or coparents, for the child. The coparents may be friends, neighbors, or people of higher social and economic status. The role of the compadres is to help the parents raise the child by paying for school books or uniforms or by providing contacts for the child when he or she needs a job.

Above: **An extended family of many generations sometimes lives together under one roof. In some households, especially in the Chocó department, women are heads of the families.**

Left: **Godparents sometimes buy candy, such as the kind this family is making, for their godchildren.**

Education

Education in Colombia has been important in maintaining sharp class distinctions. Traditionally, only the most well-to-do males were allowed to attend school. The less privileged and women were left out. When education was gradually opened to the masses, there continued to be a split between the rich and the poor in terms of the types of schools they attended. Colombians have always attached more value to skilled jobs than to manual labor, so purely academic schools were attended by the privileged, while vocational schools were attended by the disadvantaged. Recent changes in the education system, however, have made primary and secondary schools more widely available to all Colombians. In fact, education is now free to all.

In spite of an increase in government spending on education, there is still a shortage of schools, especially secondary schools, across Colombia. Generally, people in the countryside are more

Below: Unlike the children on the opposite page, this well-to-do Colombian girl attends a school with good facilities.

Left: An improvised classroom in a rain forest is actually a hut built on stilts. Despite the lack of schools in some rural areas, Colombia has a literacy rate of 92.5 percent for those over fifteen years of age.

affected by this shortage. Some parents send their children to the nearest town or city to be educated. Many, however, find the financial burden to do so too heavy. Fortunately, since the 1980s, things have taken a turn for the better in education policy.

The Colombian national government began taking responsibility for public schools. It also started devoting more money to building schools, so that no Colombian would be deprived of a chance to be educated. Although not all Colombian children have equal access to an education, the new trend encourages the less privileged to send their children to schools by making the schools affordable and accessible. Another trend is that more and more women are now attending secondary school and then going on to complete a university education.

Health Care

As with education, Colombians living in cities and large towns have much greater access to nurses, doctors, and hospitals than those living in the countryside. The state pays for some public health services, but the system does not cover the poorest workers. They either have to use their own hard-earned money or wait for sporadic visits by public health care workers for treatment.

THE DILEMMA

Doctors and nurses like to work in the cities, in either public or private hospitals, because they can make more money there than in the countryside. Because studying for a medical degree is expensive and takes many years, students prefer to work in well-paying jobs after graduation, leaving about 20 percent of the population with no access to medical professionals. As with education, the government has made serious efforts, since the 1980s, to improve the health care situation. It has built more clinics and hospitals and has increased the number of university programs in medicine.

Religion

Almost all Colombians belong to the Roman Catholic faith, which is Christianity that predates Protestant Christian denominations. In the constitution of 1886, Roman Catholicism was made the official religion of Colombia, and the church controlled such things as marriage and the education of indigenous peoples. The Colombian Roman Catholic Church is recognized as one of the most traditional of all the churches in South America, most of which are also Roman Catholic.

In 1887, the government and the church signed a concordat, or agreement, that made specifications about the Colombian government. In 1973, another concordat was signed. Under this agreement, the church lost its stronghold on the territories occupied by the Indians as well as its right to control the school curriculum. In addition, civil marriages were allowed. The government took more responsibility for indigenous peoples by providing state education and health care. Universities and public schools were allowed to teach what they wanted, and they could decide not to teach religion in the schools. It also became legal for Colombians to be married by a justice of the peace, without a church wedding. Divorce, however, was only possible outside the church, provided there was no religious wedding.

BOGOTÁ: CITY OF HOLY FAITH

Bogotá is a city of contrasts. It has modern buildings and beautiful churches and museums, as well as shantytowns. Go back in history to learn how this capital got its name.
(A Closer Look, page 46)

Below: Cali is a lively urban city in southwestern Colombia. It centers around the Plaza de Caicedo, which has churches, such as the cathedral shown here, and new museums.

The constitution of 1991 ended the 1973 agreement, and the privileges of the church were transferred to civil society. Despite these changes, the Roman Catholic Church has remained a strong force in the daily lives of Colombians. The local church is the center of activity in any small town, and priests are highly esteemed members of their communities.

Above: **These girls walk beside their mothers for their First Communion, which is an important occasion among Roman Catholics.**

People of Other Faiths

The minority of non-Catholics living in Colombia include a small population of Jews and some Protestants. Jews once lived mostly in the larger cities, but their numbers dwindled as a result of migration to other countries, especially after the political violence of the 1980s. As in other South American countries, Protestants have been successful in converting indigenous peoples to Christianity. Missionaries work in the remote areas of Colombia and provide education and health care to people whom the government has not been able to help.

Language and Literature

Spanish and Colombian Spanish

The official and most widely spoken language in Colombia is Spanish — a language that derives much of its grammar and vocabulary from Latin, the language of the Roman Empire. Spanish was the language of the Europeans who conquered most of South America, including Colombia. Although some native peoples have retained their languages successfully, many now speak Spanish. The Spanish alphabet is similar to the English one, except for three extra letters: *ch*, which sounds like the "ch" in the English word *chat*; *ll,* which sounds like "y," so *calle* (street) is pronounced CAH-yey; and *ñ*, which sounds like "n" followed by "y," so *mañana* (tomorrow) is pronounced mahn-YAH-nah. There are a few other differences in the pronunciation of Spanish letters, but, unlike English, Spanish is easy to learn because words are written exactly the way they are pronounced.

Left: **A shop by the street in Medellín, capital of Antioquia, sells both Colombian and international magazines and papers.**

Although nearly everyone speaks Spanish in modern Colombia, they do not all speak it the same way. People from Antioquia do not sound the same as those from Cauca or as those from the Caribbean coast. Differences show up in the speech between country and city dwellers, too. Social class and education also affect people's command of the vocabulary and the way they use the language.

The Literary Scene

Since Colombia gained independence from Spain, its literature has slowly matured to be among the most exciting on the continent. Since the early twentieth century, some Colombian literature has been translated into English. In 1935, José Eustacio Riviera's book *La Vorágine*, which describes one man's struggle to survive in the Amazon jungle, was published in English. It received international acclaim. Another contemporary writer with a wide readership outside Colombia is Gabriel García Márquez. Known in Colombia as "Gabo," he is perhaps the most famous writer to emerge from present-day South America.

GABO: A COLOMBIAN CERVANTES

Gabriel García Márquez, or "Gabo," put Colombia on the literary map when he received the Nobel Prize for Literature in 1982. Such is the influence of his novels that the first image many foreigners have of South America is the Caribbean coast of Colombia.
(A Closer Look, page 60)

Opposite: **Many Colombians frequent bookstores or bookfairs. Colombia publishes a wide selection of entertaining, affordable books, which can be purchased from these stores and fairs.**

Arts

All forms of artistic expression in Colombia reflect the country's diverse cultural background. Indian, Spanish, and African influences have produced unique blends in both the visual and performing arts, as well as in crafts.

Art in pre-Columbian times was varied because each indigenous group had its own unique style. The stone sculptures at San Agustín, for instance, were abstract representations of people or animals carved by a mysterious civilization. Perhaps the most famous Colombian indigenous crafts are gold jewelry and religious art. Gold was used to make nose rings, bracelets, and breastplates, as well as figures of humans and animals for religious rituals. The Gold Museum in Bogotá has the best collection of these artifacts on the continent.

From the time of the Spanish conquest of Colombia to the twentieth century, Spanish culture greatly influenced Colombian painting and sculpture. This influence was also felt in architecture and city planning, which were based on Spanish patterns. Every

Below: **A popular art market in Cali attracts both Colombians and tourists.**

Above: **A sculpture at the Santillana Center in Medellín breaks the monotony of the city's skyscrapers.**

city and town was designed on a grid pattern with a main open square in the center. The church and government buildings were built on the square. Houses were usually two stories high with patios in the center and balconies. As with painting and sculpture, Spanish styles were predominant until the beginning of the twentieth century. Architecture was not modernized until after World War II. Since then, cities, such as Medellín and Bogotá, have built modern downtown areas with skyscrapers alongside the older colonial sections of town.

Since the 1930s, Colombia has been known for producing great artists. The three most well-known painters are Enrique Grau, Alejandro Obregón, and Fernando Botero. Grau, a painter and sculptor, is famous for figurative work done in a realistic way. Obregón painted Colombian people and landscapes using large brush strokes. Although he claimed to be self-taught, Obregón studied art in France, England, and the United States. He also used falcons and flowers as symbols of Colombia. He died in 1992. Botero's work can be found in many parts of the world. His art is unique because his human and animal figures are always fat.

BOTERO'S ART: A VERY ORIGINAL POINT OF VIEW

Botero paints fat people, animals, and angels. His work has won him praise in Colombia and abroad. His is a body of work that defies conventional standards of beauty.
(A Closer Look, page 49)

Left: Participants in a music festival sing a song while playing a drum and a guitar.

Music: An Eclectic Mix

Traditional indigenous music uses only percussion and wind instruments, including a variety of drums and many types of flutes made of reeds and bamboo. Typical Colombian music can be grouped according to the main influences that define it. African Colombians, for example, brought with them drums and different beats. The *cumbia* (COOM-bee-ah), a popular musical style and dance, has a strong African influence. Along with stringed instruments, such as the guitar, the Spaniards introduced different rhythms. The *bambuco* (bahm-BOO-koh) and *torbellino* (tor-bayl-YEE-noh) are derived from indigenous music with a Spanish influence on the instrumentation. Modern music reflects influences from outside Colombia as well. Both salsa from the Caribbean and tango from Argentina are popular forms of modern music. These types of music are accompanied by specific dance steps, some of which are very complicated and exhilarating to watch.

Above: Parents who can afford the fees usually send their children for singing, dancing, or music lessons at a young age.

Crafts Galore

Many crafts developed in pre-Columbian days, as well as those developed during the colonial period, still exist. Basketry is done in most parts of the country, although different materials and patterns characterize the art of each area. Fibers from agave, cactus, palms, and bamboo are used to create beautiful and useful objects. Indigenous peoples in the Chocó area weave baskets so fine and tight they can hold water. Cloth weaving is also a traditional craft, and the woolen *ruanas* (roo-AH-nahs) of Cundinamarca are a noted example of this craft.

Limited Only by the Imagination

Colombians use almost any material to make useful and artistic crafts. Mompós, a town on the Magdalena River, is known for its beautiful gold filigree jewelry. Gold is stretched and rolled in a special way to make very fine wire, which is then twisted into intricate shapes. The Cuna Indians near the Panamanian border make decorative textile panels, called *molas* (MOH-lahs), for their clothing. Fabric of different colors is cut and sewn together by hand to create bright, abstract images of people and animals. Antioquia is famous for leatherwork, especially the shoulder bags traditionally used by mule drivers to carry their possessions.

Below: **Pottery is found all over Colombia in a variety of forms and styles. Certain areas specialize in painted, decorative pottery, while others make items for everyday use out of red and black clay. Some areas, such as the small town of Ráquira in Boyacá, depend on pottery production as their main source of employment.**

Leisure and Festivals

Chess: An Enthralling Game for Two

The most popular game in Colombia is chess. Unlike many countries, where chess is supported by the government, Colombians learn their chess skills with no public support. Nevertheless, they are the recognized chess champions of South America. The country is known for sending skilled players to the Chess Olympiads.

Other Colombian Pastimes

For Colombians with access to television, a major form of entertainment is the *telenovela* (tay-lay-noh-VAY-lah), a type of television program similar to an American soap opera, except it does not go on indefinitely. For instance, it might recount the story of a particular family and its problems only for a few months. The program is televised the same time each day or week, and people can become so involved with the program that they might alter their social schedules to accommodate it.

Below: **Both young and old enjoy the game of chess. Here, two friends are playing, while a third friend watches with interest.**

When Colombians want to party, they organize a *rumba* (ROOM-bah), which is a gathering of friends, at someone's house, to eat, drink, and dance into the wee hours of the morning. With such diverse music and dance forms in the country, the rumba is quite a popular activity among young people. In major cities and towns, movies provide evening entertainment. Due to the widespread marketing of Hollywood productions in the country, Colombians go to the same movies as their North American counterparts. Quieter forms of entertainment involve meeting friends or relatives to enjoy a meal or to chat.

Above: **Beauty pageants in Colombia are very competitive. The most important annual pageant takes place in Cartagena.**

The biggest cities, such as Bogotá and Medellín, boast a wide variety of cultural events, including theatrical performances, concerts, and art exhibitions. These events are largely restricted to the privileged, who have both the time and money to enjoy them and better access to the places where they are staged. There are also lots of lively restaurants and clubs for Colombians to frequent on weekends.

Although neither a sport nor a game, beauty pageants, seen as a means to fame and fortune, are a popular pastime among some Colombian women. Luz Marina Zuluaga won the title of Miss Universe in 1958, and, in 1992, Paola Turbay was the first runner-up.

Soccer: The King of Sports

Like their South and Central American neighbors, Colombians are big soccer fans. Most Colombian boys and some girls play soccer for sheer enjoyment, although a few boys make a career of it when they grow up. Soccer is the world's most popular sport in terms of the number of people playing and watching it. It is a simple game that demands superb fitness and little equipment — just a ball and a net. In Colombia, soccer matches draw thousands of enthusiastic spectators. The game also has personalities, such as Carlos Valderrama, the Colombian team captain for the 1998 World Cup finals in France. He is known for his soccer skills as well as his outrageous hair, and he retired in 1994. Colombian teams have participated in both the World Cup (held every four years) and the Pan-American Games. A growing number of Colombians have also taken up games popular in the United States, especially baseball and basketball. A league of women's basketball teams represents the different departments of the country.

Left: **Carlos Valderrama, unmistakable with his big hair, fights for control of the ball during the World Cup match held in France in June 1998.**

Colombia is noted for sports other than soccer, too. For a relatively small country, it has done well in international and regional sports competitions. Cycling, for example, is very popular, and Colombian cyclists have been successful in a variety of competitions, such as the World Cup and the Tour de France. Boxing is a favorite spectator sport, and boxers Kid Pambelé and Rodrigo Valdés have put Colombia on the map. A sport introduced by the Spaniards that is still practiced today is bullfighting. Bogotá has a bullring that attracts thousands of fans to every event.

Above: **Colombians love the beach. The country has many beaches for Colombians to enjoy with family or friends. They find it a great way to relax, as well as to get a tan.**

The Allure of the Water

Many Colombians enjoy water sports. Fishing is a favorite pursuit all year round, but international fishing competitions are held in Barranquilla in May and November. Swimming, waterskiing, scuba diving, and snorkeling are exciting recreational activities in the inlets and bays of the Pacific. The Rosario Islands off Cartagena are great for skin diving, but only the very brave venture there because of the danger posed by visiting sharks and barracuda.

LA CORRIDA

Most cities and towns with bullrings have bullfights. Although bullfights occur all year round, they peak in February and December, when top matadors from Spain and Colombia show off their skills in the sport. Spanish matadors are a major attraction for the local crowds.
(A Closer Look, page 62)

A Dazzling Display of Light

Holy Week starts on Palm Sunday, a week before Easter. The city of Popayán is famous for its Holy Week processions and rituals. Churches are cleaned, floors are polished, and special processions take place throughout the week. Tuesday night starts the evening candlelight processions that, from the hills around the town, look like long fiery snakes winding through the streets. The Popayán celebrations are spectacular and have been held since 1558. In the past, even civil wars were stopped so the people of Popayán could celebrate Holy Week.

A Colorful Catholic Festival

Corpus Christi is a celebration of the Eucharist, or Holy Communion, that takes place all across Colombia. Religious groups and neighborhoods work together constructing fantastic altars to decorate the streets. Every group tries to make the most beautiful altar. They use simple materials, such as silver paper, flowers, and inexpensive cloth, to reproduce scenes and objects from the Bible, such as the cup from which Christ drank. Some of the creations are truly amazing.

CARNIVAL OF BARRANQUILLA

For this event, some men dress up as birds, while others dress up as women — for fun. Their fancy costumes and dance routines amuse the hundreds of people who come to watch the performances. *(A Closer Look, page 50)*

Below: **A Holy Week procession lights up the night sky.**

Christmas: "Guess who I am?"

"Shouted Christmas Presents" is a game played in the Cauca River valley on Christmas Eve. It requires two teams. Two leaders agree to play the game and assemble their teams with people all of the same build. Everyone on the team wears the same costume, and the teams meet at an appointed time and place, where the leaders try to identify each other without speaking. The first to succeed wins the game. Then the losing team hosts a party for the winners.

Above: **In some schools, children, with the help of their teachers, make decorations, such as Santa Claus face masks, for Christmas.**

Independence Celebrations

July 20th is Colombian Independence Day. It marks the first uprising against the Spaniards. On this day, schoolchildren and military units march through the main streets of their towns and villages. In the afternoon, people watch sports events and sing patriotic folk songs. At night, dancers perform in the capital. August 7th marks the 1819 victory of Bolívar's and Santander's army against the Spaniards, who had taken back part of Colombia after the initial independence movement.

DAY OF THE BLACKS AND DAY OF THE WHITES

These two days are pure fun. You can throw flour or smear shoe polish on the faces of friends or strangers. What a novel way to make new friends!

(A Closer Look, page 56)

Food

Meal Patterns

Colombians eat three meals a day, but, unlike North Americans, their biggest meal is lunch, not dinner. Breakfast is usually small and accompanied by coffee. Lunch is always two or more courses, including a bowl of soup; a main dish of meat, fish, or poultry; and, sometimes, dessert. The preference is to eat this meal with the family, but, in urban areas on weekdays, a family lunch is often difficult, so every city and town has a number of restaurants and cafeterias that specialize in serving the lunchtime meal. The evening meal usually follows the same pattern of soup and a main course, but the main course is often smaller when eaten at home and soup is sometimes omitted. Staple starches are rice, potatoes, corn, plantains, and yucca. People in southern regions, near Ecuador, eat more potatoes than other starches. Meat is more common in highland areas; fish is eaten more often on the coasts. Over the past decade, however, there has been a trend toward vegetarian food. There are not many vegetarian restaurants in the country, but they are slowly increasing in number.

COFFEE, ANYONE?

This beverage is consumed hot or cold by about one-third of the world's population. Together with Brazil, Colombia satisfies most of the world's demand for coffee. Thus, the coffee crop makes an important contribution to the Colombian economy. *(A Closer Look, page 54)*

Below: **Some homemakers in Colombia buy live chickens at the market.**

Food That Whets Your Appetite

Some popular main dishes in Colombia are grilled beef, stewed beef with sauce, chicken with rice, and grilled fish. In coastal areas, rice is sometimes cooked with coconut milk, which gives it a slightly sweet taste. Around Bogotá, a very popular soup is *ajiaco santafereño* (ah-hee-AH-koh sahn-tah-fay-RAYN-yoh), which is made from avocados, chicken, corn on the cob, and capers. In the south, people enjoy *locros de choclos* (LOH-krohs day CHOH-klohs), a soup made from corn and potatoes. People in San Andrés and Providencia eat *rondón* (rohn-DOHN), a soup made from fish, shellfish, coconut milk, yucca, and plantains. Perhaps the food most enjoyed in all of Colombia is *arepas* (ah-REE-pahs), or cornbread. For dessert, there is an abundance of fresh fruits and sweets made from milk. Market stalls and traveling vendors sell a wide variety of snacks, including cheese buns; *empanadas* (aym-pah-NAH-dahs), which are pastries stuffed with meat and vegetables; *buñuelos* (boon-yoo-AY-lohs), which are deep-fried balls of dough and cheese; and yucca bread.

JUICE UP YOUR LIFE

Many types of fruits are available in Colombia. Some of the more familiar fruits from which juices are made are bananas, pineapples, mangoes, and passion fruit. Colombia has many other types; for example, star apples (which have the shape of a star when cut across), marmalade plums, honey berries, tree tomatoes, and *guanabana* (gwah-NAH-bah-nah). A guanabana is green, warty, and ugly on the outside but white and delicious on the inside. Colombia produces its own soft drinks and many varieties of beer. The favorite liquor is *aguardiente* (ah-gwahr-dee-AYN-tay), made from sugarcane or honey. It is sometimes combined with hot coffee or cinnamon to make a warm drink.

A CLOSER LOOK AT COLOMBIA

Colombia lies at the gateway to South America, which means the continent's first inhabitants passed through Colombia as they moved south. In the late thirteenth century, Spaniards, guided by the dream of *El Dorado*, or a country rich in gold and other treasures, came to Colombia. Over the years, the country yielded riches but not in the quantities the Spaniards wanted. Some took the riches back home; others stayed. Some of the Spaniards who settled in Colombia married the Indians and blacks there. These intermarriages gave rise to the ethnic blend characteristic of Colombia today.

This section will familiarize you with the things that make Colombia unique. Many people think of Colombia as a country of drug lords and guerillas and not much else. With a closer look, however, the picture is quite different. From the emerald mines in Muzo and Chivor to the ancient stone sculptures at San Agustín, from historic Magdalena to the Spanish fortress of Cartagena, or from colorful festivals to vibrant cities, such as Bogotá, Colombia's diversity will fascinate any visitor to the country.

Opposite: **Most Colombians from the llanos, such as this typical cowboy, raise cattle for a living.**

Below: **In countryside and small-town cafés, older Colombians sometimes play cards with friends after a meal.**

Afro-Colombians: The Third Branch

If you think of Colombian culture as a tree with three main branches, the first would be labeled indigenous, the second Spanish, and the third African. Many Africans were brought to the New World as slaves. In South America, Spanish colonists relied on native peoples for mining and farming, but, when disease and abuse significantly reduced their numbers, the colonists used Africans. From the 1500s until the abolition of slavery in 1850, Africans were used across the continent as miners, farmers, and servants. In colonial Colombia, the largest numbers of slaves were found on the Caribbean coast and in the mines near Antioquia.

Not all South American slaves accepted their fate easily. Some managed to escape and, as free people, established their own communities. In Colombia, the communities were called *palenques* (pah-LAYN-kays), which means "wooden stockades." This word was appropriate because slaves who escaped had to defend their freedom — sometimes with their lives.

Below: **Many Afro-Colombians work in timber extraction industries, on coffee plantations, and in mines.**

The earliest palenque community in the area once considered Colombia was established in Panama in 1556. In 1634, a group of palenques united under a former slave woman, Queen Leonor, and declared themselves independent of the Spanish crown. This declaration was the first effort toward freedom from Spanish rule in all of Colombia. Unfortunately, the governor at Cartagena, fearing that Queen Leonor and her followers would encourage a massive slave rebellion, sent troops to kill the rebels. One town near Cartagena is still called San Basilio de Palenque, pointing to the town's origins as a haven for escaped slaves.

Although all Colombians live together in legal freedom and equality, racism still exists and especially affects those with darker skin. Before the 1991 constitution came into effect, Afro-Colombians asked to be formally recognized as a separate cultural group. They asked for protection against discrimination and legal rights to their lands (as was guaranteed for indigenous peoples). The assembly that drew up the constitution did not include these demands, suggesting that Congress consider them later. In 1993, Congress responded by designating two seats for Afro-Colombian representatives. This decision marked the beginning of a formal recognition of Colombia's African heritage.

Above: **The Afro-Colombian family structure is different from that of other Colombians, except in some Indian groups. Afro-Colombians, especially those in the Chocó department, practice polygamy.**

Bogotá: City of Holy Faith

Santa Fé de Bogotá, commonly referred to as Bogotá, is both an old and a new name for Colombia's capital city. In 1537, Gonzalo Jiménez de Quesada, a *conquistador* (cohn-KEES-tah-dohr), or Spanish conqueror, found a basin, nestled in the mountains, that was settled by Chibcha Indians. The Spaniards fought the Indians for control, and, in 1538, they founded the city.

The full name of the city is *Santa Fé de Bogotá del Nuevo Reino de Granada de las Indias del Mar Océano.* Each part of this long name reflects something characteristic of this Spanish conquest in South America. *Santa Fé* refers to the Spaniards being devout Catholics. Part of their mission in the New World was to convert indigenous peoples to Christianity, or Holy Faith. Bogotá was the Spanish interpretation of "Bacatá," which is what the Chibchas called their settlement. *Nuevo Rieno de Granada* means "New Kingdom of Granada." There is an area in Spain called Granada, and this part of the New World was thought to be an extension of the territories controlled by the King of Spain. The phrase *de las Indias*

Below: **The cathedral on the Plaza Bolívar in Bogotá stands where the first mass was celebrated after the city was founded in 1538.**

Left: **At night, the capital city of Bogotá is illuminated by the lights from its many buildings and skyscrapers. Bogotá is the largest city in Colombia, with a number of neighborhoods that have grown around the old colonial core, La Candelaria. It is also the center of a lively arts and music scene. At an altitude of 8,660 feet (2,640 m), Bogotá has a cool, rainy climate comparable to London, England. Some residents of Bogotá, called *cachacos* (kah-CHAH-kohs), are famous for their poetry and sophisticated wit.**

means "of the Indies." The New World was originally called the Indies because Columbus thought he was in the Indies when he first arrived in the Caribbean. Finally, the phrase *del Mar Océano* means "of the Ocean Sea."

Throughout the colonial period, the capital of the region known as New Granada was Santa Fé. Here, in 1810, the wars for independence from Spain gained their momentum. Parts of Colombia declared independence, but full independence came after Simón Bolívar and his men defeated Spain in 1819. The name of the capital city was subsequently changed to Bogotá.

In the nineteenth century and the first half of the twentieth century, Bogotá was known as the "Athens of South America," because its residents were well educated and famous for their poetry. Although Bogotá was the capital of the new country, it was too far away from the real centers of population and commerce on the coast and in Medellín, so the name Bogotá came to be used for any place far away and isolated. In 1954, Bogotá became part of a special district separate from other municipal governments. In 1991, the new constitution changed the name of that district to "Capital District" and gave the city its old name, Santa Fé de Bogotá.

Botero's Art: A Very Original Point of View

The Beginning

Fernando Botero was born in Medellín in 1932. He first worked as a writer and illustrator for a Medellín newspaper, *El Colombiano*. In 1951, at the age of nineteen, he held his first one-man show in Bogotá. The following year, he went to Europe to study in Madrid, Spain, and Florence, Italy. Botero lived in Florence until 1955, studying fresco and art history, which have influenced his paintings ever since. When he returned to Bogotá in 1955, his work was not well received, but Botero did not give up.

The Break

Over the next twenty years, Botero moved from Bogotá to Mexico City to New York to Paris. In the 1960s, his work began to receive positive attention. For example, in 1961, the Museum of Modern Art in New York bought one of his paintings, *Mona Lisa at Age 12*. Exhibitions of his work were held in Germany, Colombia, the Netherlands, the United States, and Venezuela. After his show in Venezuela, the Venezuelan government awarded him the Order of Andrés Bello, which is reserved for outstanding figures in Latin American culture. Botero has also been honored at home. The Colombian government awarded him the Cruz de Boyacá for his contributions to the country.

Above: **This boy has taken shelter under Botero's *Fat Lady* sculpture.**

Source of Botero's Inspiration

Botero's art is inspired by his vision of Colombia and Colombians. It is distinctive because his figures, whether children, adults, animals, or angels, are always portrayed as incredibly fat. His paintings might seem funny at first glance, but on closer inspection, they are often social commentaries with serious political overtones.

Botero was featured in the first issue of *Latin American Art*, a magazine published in the United States. It used one of his paintings — an armored angel with scenery from a Colombian village in the background — on the cover. Once you've seen a Botero, you'll never mistake his work for anyone else's!

Opposite: **The striking thing about Botero's work is that all his sculptures are fat.**

Carnival of Barranquilla

All Colombia participates in the festivities of Carnival, and the celebration in Barranquilla, called the Carnival of Barranquilla, is the most famous. This city starts preparing for Carnival just after Christmas, and for the two months preceding Lent, the public square is filled with masquerades and dancing.

The traditions of Carnival go back many centuries to the first human settlements on the northern coast of Colombia. Carnival holidays, which originated in Europe, were brought to the Americas by the Spaniards and Portuguese. The Carnival of Barranquilla has its nearest origins in the Cartagena de Indians festivities during the colonial period. It was then a feast for slaves, when the Africans, dressed in special costumes and playing indigenous instruments, roamed the city singing and dancing.

In Cartagena, the traditional Novena de la Candelaria was the background for sumptuous balls in the eighteenth century. During this time, a holiday was granted to black slaves who had

Below: **This dancer, in her glittering costume, performs with others as she makes her way down the streets during Carnival.**

50

recently landed from Africa. The main dances of the Barranquilla Carnival were first performed during these holidays.

Unique Dances

Several ritual dances are performed during Carnival. The maestranza is a comical dance for which men dress up as women. In another dance, also performed by men, participants wear costumes that look like bird plumage and masks with beaks. The coyongo is a ritual dance-drama. A coyongo is an aquatic fishing bird, and in this dance, several birdmen circle around a man dressed as a fish. The man, in turn, tries to dodge the "birds" closing in on him.

In 1967, a new event, called the Grand Parade, was introduced. It takes place on Sunday, the second day of Carnival. In 1974, following the initiative of Esther Forero, a famous singer and composer, the first Guacherna was held. Dancers using popular instruments went from house to house looking for more dancers to join them. Today, Carnival still has a Mardi Gras atmosphere to it.

Above and *below:* **Mummies come alive during Carnival! People often dress up in special costumes or as animals to thrill the many spectators who gather to watch.**

Cartagena: Gateway to the Caribbean

Cartagena was founded in 1533. During the colonial period, it was one of only three ports used by the Spaniards to ship their riches back to Europe. Because pirates from other countries were always on the lookout for ships filled with gold and silver, only one major shipment, heavily guarded by warships, left Cartagena each year. For the rest of the year, piles of treasure lay in the city, making Cartagena a target for English privateers (pirates) who were enemies of Spain at that time. The King of Spain paid large sums of money to build huge fortifications around the city. At one point, there were twenty-nine forts and bastions in and around the old walled city.

In its heyday, Cartagena was a center of colonial life and trade. Ironically, this hub of the Spanish Empire was the second city in South America to declare its independence from Europe. In November 1811, the city supported Venezuelan Simón Bolívar and brimmed with revolutionary activity. It was retaken by

Left: **Las Bovedas in Cartagena were built two centuries ago as dungeons with very thick walls. Today, they are one of the major tourist attractions in the city.**

Spanish soldiers under Pablo Morillo in 1815, but the 1811 declaration still marks a time of celebration in Cartagena.

Above: **Thousands crowd the streets during the procession of the Candelaria Virgin from La Popa Convent.**

Candlemas, or Candelaria, is another important festival in Cartagena. Traditionally, the candles used in churches are blessed on this day. The Virgin of Candelaria is the patron saint of Cartagena, so this day has special meaning for the city's residents. The celebration starts nine days before February 2, when people climb La Popa, the highest hill in the city and the site of an old convent church. The processions up the hill are lit by the candles people carry with them for the Virgin. At the foot of the hill, people dance the cumbia with lighted candles, sometimes all night long.

Cartagena is Colombia's main tourist city. It is famous for the beauty of the surviving colonial architecture and for its relaxed atmosphere. Because it was the first slave port in the New World, the people and culture are a mix of European and African influences. After independence, new waves of immigrants arrived to further mix and meld the culture of Cartagena. It is little wonder, then, that Colombians from other areas, as well as foreigners, visit this vibrant Caribbean port in large numbers.

Coffee, Anyone?

Although oil is the major export in Colombia, people more often associate the country with coffee. Coffee is one of Colombia's major agricultural exports. It has been crucial to the country's industrialization throughout the twentieth century. Colombia is second only to Brazil as a coffee producer in South America, and at times, coffee has represented about 60 percent of the country's export earnings.

The Origins of Coffee

Today, we take coffee for granted, but a few hundred years ago, it was a novelty. Coffee drinking began in the Middle East and slowly spread to Europe in the 1600s. At first, the only reliable source of coffee was a place in Yemen called Al Mukha (origin of the word "mocha"). In the early 1700s, the Dutch brought coffee to Java (part of Indonesia) and started exporting huge quantities

Left: **In its wild state, the coffee shrub is an evergreen bush. Its branches bear small, white, sweet-smelling flowers, and its fruit, which is red when mature, is called a cherry. The cherry consists of a fleshy pulp and two seeds.**

Above: **Before coffee beans reach the stores, farmers sell them to distributors who take pains to select the best.**

back to Europe. The institution of the "coffee house" became widespread in Europe in the 1700s and 1800s. In the 1880s, when Javanese coffee was affected by a fungus that wiped out the plantations, coffee production started to boom in South America. The first country to enter into large-scale coffee production was Brazil. By the early twentieth century, however, coffee production had spread to Colombia, Costa Rica, and other parts of Central America.

Coffee beans are the seeds of a coffee plant, which is a perennial shrub that grows in rich soils and in climates with evenly distributed rainfall. The climate also has to be frost-free and temperate. A coffee plant's life span is twenty to forty years, and it might produce different quantities of seeds each year. The ripened fruits, or cherries, are processed by separating the coffee seeds from their coverings and the pulp and by drying the seeds. Then, they are roasted to different degrees. The next time you buy coffee, look for labels that say "dark," "medium," or "light" roast. The type of bean and the degree of roasting determines the flavor of the coffee. Coffee is produced in the departments of Antioquia, Santander, Cundinamarca, Caldas, Risaralda, Quindío, Tolima, and Valle del Cauca.

DIFFERENT TYPES OF COLOMBIAN COFFEE

In Colombia, you can order three different types of coffee: simple, black coffee; milky coffee; and milk with coffee, which is a cup of frothy hot milk with a little bit of coffee for flavor. As in many parts of the world, coffee break in Colombia is a time to relax and enjoy the company of friends.

Day of the Blacks and Day of the Whites

In Popayán, two very unique festivals are held after the Christmas season. On January 5th, people celebrate Day of the Blacks, or Día De Negritos, and on January 6th, they celebrate Day of the Whites, or Fiesta De Los Blanquitos. These bizarre, colorful festivals evolved from pagan rituals in pre-Columbian times. Later, the rituals underwent some minor changes due to Spanish influences.

Black Faces

On the morning of Day of the Blacks, boys with shoe polish chase girls and do not give up until they smear the polish on the girls' faces. By evening, if you are out on the streets, you cannot escape some type of "decoration" on your face, hands, or body. So, some

Below: **During Day of the Blacks, no one will stare at you if you are walking around with a black face. If you have a clean face, however, you had better run for cover!**

people just stay home on this day. In the afternoon, there are street parades, with people in masquerade and strolling musicians playing the latest bambucos, and in the main square, wealthy farmers make donations of food. The celebration continues at a club or a home late into the night.

Partying with Total Abandon

January 6th is the direct opposite of January 5th — and the focus is on white. Again, boys chase girls, but, this time, with flour. Young people literally paint the town white. They throw flour at friends and strangers' faces or spray them with talcum powder. Even the police are not let off easily, but they take it in good spirit, all in the name of fun. Talcum spraying can be dated quite accurately to a specific incident in 1912 when a man snatched a woman's powder puff and playfully dusted his friends' faces. Those who live in apartments with balconies throw water mixed with flour over people walking in the street, who might already have flour on them. Mixing together flour, talcum powder, and water has made Day of the Whites a very sticky affair. Because of the mess, people do not wear their best clothes on this day.

Below: **Some people cannot decide whether to go all black or all white, so they mix both colors.**

Emeralds: Colombia's Green Treasure

Emeralds are among the most expensive precious stones in the world, and the very best emeralds are mined in Muzo and Chivor to the north and northeast of Bogotá.

Emeralds were used in pre-Columbian jewelry and thrown into Lake Guatavita in the Andes as ceremonial offerings to indigenous gods. Since the Spanish conquest of Colombia, the country's emeralds have circled the globe. Spaniards took the emeralds in large numbers to Europe. From there, they were sold to the rulers of India. Later, the Persians (modern-day Iranians) invaded India and took many treasures back to the Middle East. Today, some of these historic Colombian emeralds are part of the crown jewels of Iran and museum collections in Turkey. Even the head of the Roman Catholic Church, the pope, wears an emerald as a symbol of his office.

Below: **Some of the best emeralds from this Colombian mine are available in Bogotá at reasonable prices.**

Emeralds are believed to possess special powers. For example, emeralds are supposed to cancel magic spells, reveal the truth, promote good health, and make a person more intelligent! Emeralds are also said to be the gem of lovers and are the traditional anniversary gift for people married fifty-five years. They are also the birthstone for people born in the month of May.

Under Spanish rule, Chivor was the historic center for emerald mining. Because the Spaniards abused Indian labor to mine emeralds, both the rulers of Spain and the Catholic Church abolished Indian slavery. The site at Chivor continues to be mined, and, in the 1970s, the Colombian government also opened Muzo to private miners. Both areas were noted for violent crime due to competition among miners. The miners now have a private contract with the government to exploit the mines, so crimes are generally reduced in number.

Good emeralds combine brilliant green color with beautiful sparkle. The best place to buy emeralds is Bogotá. Colombians also travel around the world selling emeralds to the finest jewelers. The next time you see an emerald, remember, it might have come all the way from Colombia!

Above: **These miners are showing off their finds. Emeralds are sold by weight using special measurements called carats and points. A carat is one-fifth of a gram, and a point is one-hundredth of a gram.**

Gabo: A Colombian Cervantes

Gabriel García Márquez, or Gabo, was born March 6, 1928, in Aracataca, a town near the Caribbean coast of Colombia. Although born in poverty, Gabo attended university in Bogotá. In 1948, his studies were interrupted by violence surrounding the assassination of Jorge Gaitán, who was running for president. Gabo then worked as a journalist in Cartagena, Barranquilla, and Bogotá. In the late 1950s, he worked as a foreign correspondent

Left: **Gabriel García Márquez is a famous Colombian writer.**

for *Bogotá Daily* in Rome and Paris. In 1955, he published his first novel, *Leaf Storm and Other Stories,* and, in 1972, it was translated into English. Since then, Gabo has published countless novels, newspaper articles, and collections of short stories.

One Hundred Years of Solitude

Gabo gained world renown in 1967 with the publication of what is probably his best work to date, *One Hundred Years of Solitude.* It was published in English in 1970. Written while he was in Mexico, it is a story about seven generations of a family living in the mythical town of Macondo, which is based on Aracataca and became the setting of most of his later stories. This book presents the history of Colombia as the backdrop for family affairs. It also recounts the history of Macondo and its founders. *One Hundred Years of Solitude* has been called the second-greatest Spanish novel after *Don Quixote*, which was written by Spanish novelist Miguel Cervantes nearly four hundred years ago.

Subsequent Novels

Since 1970, Gabo has had a large international following of readers, and, now, his novels and short stories are translated into English within a year of their Spanish publication. His most recent novels are *Love in the Time of Cholera* (1988), a love story set in Cartagena; *The General In His Labyrinth* (1990), a fictional account of Simón Bolívar during the last months of his life; and *Of Love and Other Demons* (1995), based on a legend about a young girl whose hair continues to grow after her death from rabies. Gabo received the Nobel Prize for Literature in 1982. He is the first Colombian ever to have received a Nobel Prize.

Key Figure in Magic Realism Movement

In Gabo's stories, events are loosely based on truth and legend but are often portrayed in a mythical or magical way. This style of combining reality and myth is known as magic realism. Many other Spanish-American writers have adopted this style but have not achieved Gabo's level of success. Some people feel that Gabo's style is similar to that of American novelist William Faulkner.

Gabo currently lives in both Mexico and Colombia and spends time in the United States.

Above: **The Spanish publication of Gabo's 1989 novel *El General En Su Laberinto* (*The General in His Labyrinth*) was followed by the English publication in 1990. The book is about Simón Bolívar. Gabo's most recent work of fiction, *News of a Kidnapping*, concerns the Colombian drug trade and was published in 1996.**

La Corrida

Bullfighting is a popular sport in Spain, Portugal, some parts of France, and Latin America. In Colombia, bullfighting, or La Corrida, takes place throughout the year. The most important bullfights, however, occur in the months of February and December, when the top matadors from Colombia and other countries, such as Spain, participate in international festivals.

Bullfighting is a dangerous sport that demands great courage, skill, and coordination. The bulls used in this sport are specially bred for specific characteristics, such as aggressive instincts, and they are usually killed in the bullring.

The Bullfight Program

In a typical program, three matadors fight two bulls each. The program begins with a procession. The matadors parade around the arena in their elaborate outfits, which include short jackets, waistcoats, skintight trousers embroidered with rich colors, dress capes, and stockings. The matadors lead the procession carrying

Below: **Because the bull must die before a matador can claim his or her prize, some people, especially animal rights activists, think bullfighting is a cruel sport that should be stopped.**

swords. Behind them are the six-man teams that assist them. By the time the procession ends, screams from the spectators have reached a crescendo. A trumpet sounds, and the bull pen opens to release the first fearsome bull.

Team members goad the bull so the matador can observe its movements. The matador then makes some passes, or moves with his cape. He swings the cape slowly away from the lunging bull without moving his feet, while, at the same time, working as close to the bull's horns as possible. The picadors, assistants to the matador who ride horseback, harass the bull by poking lances, or barbed sticks, into its shoulders. The banderilleros, assistants on foot who work with the cape, follow by thrusting decorative darts into the bull's neck or shoulders.

In the final act, the matador reenters the ring and makes some passes to prepare the bull for the kill. The crowd encourages him with appreciative cheers, especially for his deft maneuvers. Then, the matador is ready for the kill. Usually, the matador stands still as the bull charges toward him. At the last minute, he steps aside and plunges a sword into the animal.

Above: **Sometimes, in a bullfight program, a matador drinks liquor made from herbs, then passes the drink to his assistants. In Spain, if the matador is well known, he circles the arena to the applause of the crowd.**

The Magdalena: Colombia's Watery Highway

The Magdalena River begins its journey to the Caribbean in the highlands between the Central and Eastern Cordilleras. It flows 956 miles (1,538 km) to Barranquilla on the Caribbean coast. The main tributary of the Magdalena is the Cauca River.

Most rivers spilling out of the Andes Mountains drop sharply in elevation, forming waterfalls that prevent ships from sailing upstream. Because the Magdalena is navigable for most of its length, it has played a significant role in Colombia's history as one of the primary forms of transportation, allowing ships to sail from the Caribbean to the Colombian highlands.

The mouth of the Magdalena was first sighted by Europeans in 1501, and in 1525, the first Colombian settlement, Santa Marta,

Below: **Ships dock in the harbor of Barranquilla, which is at the mouth of the Magdalena River. Barranquilla is Colombia's main seaport.**

was established nearby. In 1536, Gonzalo Jiménez de Quesada's expedition sailed up the Magdalena to a place near modern Barrancabermeja before setting off inland on foot. Since the founding of Bogotá as the capital of the new Spanish province, the Magdalena has been the primary route used to ship goods between the highlands and the coast. In the beginning, canoes made by indigenous peoples and keelboats were used to transport goods. By the mid-1840s, the first steam-powered boats were in use. These boats relied on wood to keep fires burning, which produced steam to power the paddle wheels. The boats stopped periodically to take on more wood, and the stopping places soon developed into small towns.

Above: **In the seventeenth century, navigation problems on the Magdalena greatly hindered Barranquilla's development. So, most goods traveling on the river passed through Cartegena. The problems were resolved by the nineteenth century.**

The Land and Air Take Over

The Magdalena continued to be Colombia's main "highway" well into the twentieth century. Now, with more roads and railroads, goods can be moved faster on land. The introduction of airplanes and the construction of runways in the last few decades has made flight the fastest way to travel. The Magdalena might not be critical to life in Colombia anymore, but without it, Colombia's history would certainly have been different.

Nature's Magicians: Butterflies

Butterflies belong to the order or group of insects known as Lepidoptera, which includes 15,000 species of butterflies and 150,000 species of moths. Butterflies are different from moths because they are most active during the day, while moths are active at night. Three thousand or 35 percent of all known butterfly species can be found in Colombia's diverse ecosystems.

A Beautiful Metamorphosis

Butterflies have a fascinating and magical life cycle. The first stage of a butterfly is the egg, which is deposited on a particular type of leaf. Each species depends on different types of plants, so butterflies are quite sensitive to ecological destruction. When the egg hatches, the larva comes out in the form of a caterpillar.

Below: **Pretty butterflies gather on a dry riverbed in the Amazon rain forest.**

Caterpillars eat the leaves they are born on and may shed their skins as they grow. They spin a support for themselves on a leaf or a twig, and attached to that, they transform into butterflies. The adult butterfly, which is also called an imago, lives on pollen and nectar from the flowers. After the adults mate, the female lays eggs, and the cycle starts all over again.

Different Forests for Different Butterflies

Three types of forests support butterflies in Colombia: the tropical rain forests, the savanna forests of eastern Colombia, and the Andean mountain forests.

The highland forests generally support dark-colored butterflies that need to absorb energy from the sun to stay alive. The tropical rain forests and savanna forests support larger and more brightly colored species of butterflies. The most famous is the Morpho, which is a large, iridescent blue butterfly. It seems to appear as if by magic, fluttering across clearings in the forest. As the sunlight catches the blue of its wings, it is as if jewels have taken flight. There are also tiger butterflies with wings striped like a tiger and countless others with a wide range of wing colors and patterns.

A GOOD SIGN

Although many species of butterflies migrate, Colombian butterflies usually do not. This is because the country is divided by high mountain chains that are not easy for butterflies to cross. Because each species of butterfly is dependent on specific types of plants for its caterpillar and imago stages, butterflies are extremely sensitive to disruptions in their ecosystem. For this reason, it is said that the presence of butterflies indicates a healthy environment.

Adapting to Changes

A group of coastal Colombians settled primarily in Chicago. Many of these people were of African or Indian descent and had found that, despite their education, it was difficult for them to succeed in Colombia due to racism. In the United States, these groups did not mix well with other ethnic groups, so the coastal population did not follow the Colombian path to Jackson Heights. Instead, they lived first in the inner city of Chicago, and, as their incomes improved, they moved to the more affluent suburbs north of the city. Colombian-Americans do not live only in these two cities. They have settled in smaller numbers all over the United States, and, wherever they live, they have made contributions to local life and society.

Colombians are different from other immigrant groups from Central and South America. Because of higher levels of education, they adapt quickly. They are also slow to become involved in politics because it was often politics that drove them from their homeland. Colombian families tend to be small, and female Colombian immigrants are more likely to work at well-paying jobs than their counterparts from Central and South America.

Below: **Many Colombian-Americans, especially teenagers, are no different from their American peers. They like the same kinds of music, actors, and even pets.**

Making a Mark on American Society

Colombian women have made their mark on American society in many different fields, including the arts and sciences. Adriana C. Ocampo, a planetary geologist, first worked for NASA after graduating from high school in Pasadena, California. Born in Barranquilla in 1955, Ocampo immigrated to the United States when she was fifteen years old. After taking a summer job at Pasadena's NASA facility during her junior year, she continued to work for NASA while completing her university degree at UCLA, Los Angeles. She was involved with Project Galileo, NASA's mission to explore Jupiter.

Colombian women have also contributed to the American arts scene. Patricia Gonzalez, born in Cartagena, studied in England and moved to Houston, Texas, in 1981. As a painter, she is known for her special style in portraying landscapes and flowers. Her style is called magic realism because her images are very dreamlike. She has exhibited her work in Houston, New York, Los Angeles, and Cartagena. She received a National Endowment for the Arts fellowship and was included in the traveling exhibit *Hispanic Art in the United States*.

Below: **Ocampo (left) is presently working with the Galileo mission to Jupiter. Professor Rodolfo Llinás (right) from the New York University School of Medicine has contributed over five hundred publications to brain research, has been awarded six honorary degrees, and is the recipient of numerous honors.**

Americans in Colombia

For many reasons, there has not been a significant movement of Americans to Colombia. The violence that has plagued Colombia over the last fifty years has been a strong deterrent to possible immigration. Recently, because of the conflicts between governments over how to handle drug dealers, Colombia has become an "unfriendly" place for Americans. One of the largest groups of visitors to Colombia from the United States is Drug Enforcement Administration (DEA) officers.

The Role of DEA Officers

The DEA is responsible for limiting drug sales in the United States. Part of that job is to try to prevent shipments of drugs, and, if possible, the production of drugs. Colombia is the world's leading grower of coca, the plant from which cocaine is made. The country is the main center of cocaine production and shipment to the United States. The drug lords do not want to face American courts, so the presence of the DEA has resulted in even more violence.

Above: **During their stays in Colombia, the families of American executives often enjoy the country's tropical climate by relaxing around a swimming pool.**

Other Americans in Colombia

Two groups of Americans that have moved to Colombia in small numbers are business people and Protestant missionaries. The first group includes the executives of American-owned industries and their families. These people often move only for the duration of their contracts, and they do not tend to form stable communities. Missionary groups are scattered in parts of Colombia. They have been coming to Colombia since the 1960s and 1970s, when various American churches sponsored missionary work in South America. The missionaries usually work with indigenous communities and try to improve their economic conditions. They also teach religion. They do not stay long in Colombia either, because they are generally sent to work in a country for a limited period of time. If the current trend toward reduction in violence continues, there may be a resurgence of tourism in Colombia.

Left: **Some American directors have used Colombia as a setting for their movies. In the movie *Romancing the Stone*, Michael Douglas and Kathleen Turner go after treasure buried in Cartagena. Douglas plays the role of a rugged adventurer, while Turner is a romantic novelist. Together, they become involved in an adventure of their own through the forests, rivers, and caves of Colombia. This movie created an interest among some Americans in visiting Colombia.**

Cultural Influences

As in many countries all over the world, there has been a great deal of American cultural influence on Colombians. For the middle and upper classes, America has been the source of fashion trends and the preferred destination for immigration. Through television and movies, Colombians are exposed to American values and ideas about living. Most Colombians do not imitate Americans in all respects, but items of clothing, such as blue jeans, are now as common in Colombian cities as they are in New York or Los Angeles. In the other direction, Colombians have had a smaller overall influence on Americans than other Hispanic groups, such as Mexicans, Puerto Ricans, and Cubans. Over time, these groups have introduced non-Hispanic Americans to elements of their culture, such as food and music. Sometimes, Colombians get lost in this larger Hispanic group. For example, a character on the popular 1980s television series, *Hill Street Blues*, Lieutenant Ray Calletano, was Colombian but was often treated as if he were Mexican or Puerto Rican.

Above: **Cumbia has a growing following in the United States. Since the 1960s and 1970s, American music has gained popularity with Colombian youths, too. "Rock" has joined the long list of rhythms that can be heard in this music-loving country.**

Providencia

San Andrés

CARIBBEAN SEA

PANAMA

Gulf of Urabá

A   B   C   D

La Guajira Peninsula

Santa Marta

LA GUAJIRA

Barranquilla

ATLÁNTICO

Cristóbal Colón
(18,947 ft / 5,775 m)

1

Cartagena

Sierra Nevada de Santa Marta

César

MAGDALENA

CÉSAR

SUCRE

CÓRDOBA

Sinú

BOLÍVAR

NORTE DE SANTANDER

Cúcuta

Cauca

Magdalena

Barrancabermeja

VENEZUELA

2

Atrato

ANTIOQUIA

SANTANDER

ARAUCA

Orinoco

Medellín

CHOCÓ

CALDAS

BOYACÁ

LLANOS

CORDILLERA OCCIDENTAL

RISARALDA

CUNDINAMARCA

CASANARE

PACIFIC

QUINDÍO

BOGOTÁ

Meta

VICHADA

N

OCEAN

3

Buenaventura

Cali

TOLIMA

CAPITAL DISTRICT

CORDILLERA CENTRAL

VALLE DEL CAUCA

CORDILLERA ORIENTAL

META

Guaviare

GUAINÍA

Popayán

HUILA

CAUCA

Tumaco

GUAVIARE

San Agustín

VAUPÉS

NARIÑO

ANDES

CAQUETÁ

Vaupés

4

PUTUMAYO

Equator

Caquetá

BRAZIL

ECUADOR

AMAZONAS

Putumayo

P E R U

5

COLOMBIA

Amazon

State Boundary

Capital

City

River

86

Above: A flowering tree brightens up a quiet town in the Cauca.

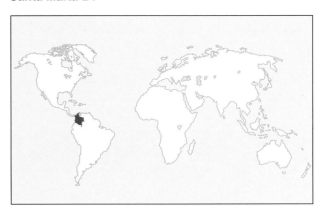

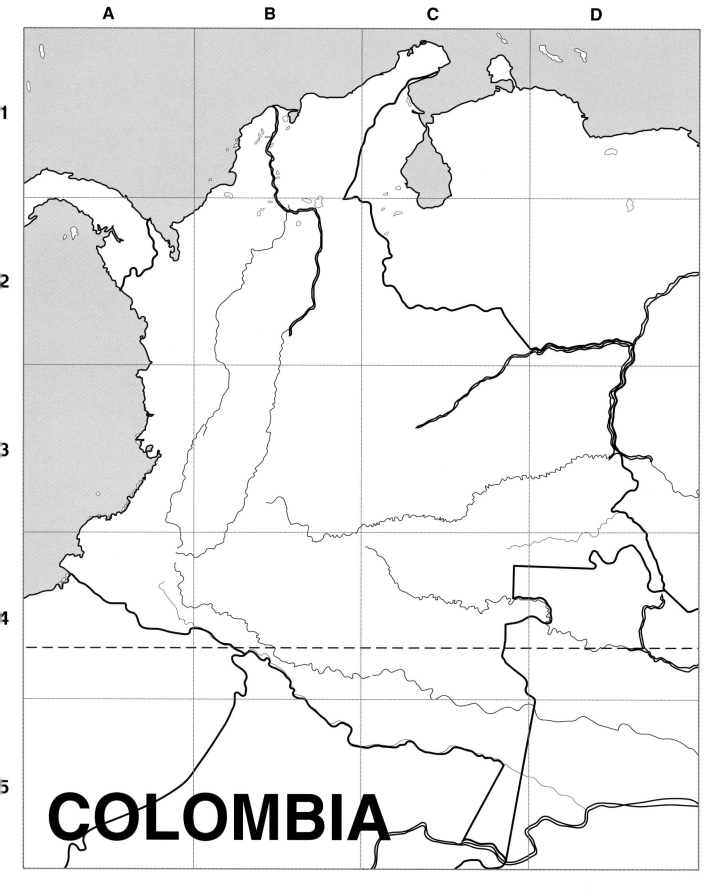

COLOMBIA

How Is Your Geography?

Learning to identify the main geographical areas and points of a country can be challenging. Although it may seem difficult at first to memorize the locations and spellings of major cities or the names of mountain ranges, rivers, deserts, lakes, and other prominent physical features, the end result of this effort can be very rewarding. Places you previously did not know existed will suddenly come to life when referred to in world news, whether in newspapers, television reports, or other books and reference sources. This knowledge will make you feel a bit closer to the rest of the world, with its fascinating variety of cultures and physical geography.

This map can be duplicated for use in a classroom. (PLEASE DO NOT WRITE IN THIS BOOK!) Students can then fill in any requested information on their individual map copies. The student can also make a copy of the map and use it as a study tool to practice identifying place names and geographical features on his or her own.

Above: **Shades of the blue sky are reflected in this lake in Colombia.**

Colombia at a Glance

Official Name República de Colombia, Republic of Colombia

Capital Bogotá

Language Spanish for the majority of the population; indigenous languages for a small minority; and English in San Andrés and Providencia

Population 42,310,775 (2004 estimate)

Land Area 440,831 square miles (1,141,752 square km)

Departments Antioquia, Atlántico, Bolívar, Boyacá, Caldas, Caquetá, Cauca, César, Chocó, Córdoba, Cundinamarca, Huila, La Guajira, Magdalena, Meta, Nariño, Norte de Santander, Quindío, Risaralda, Santander, Sucre, Tolima, Valle del Cauca

Highest Point Cristóbal Colón 18,947 feet (5,775 m)

Major Rivers Amazon, Atrato, Magdalena, Orinoco, Sinú

Longest River Magdalena River

Main Religion Roman Catholicism

Current President Alvaro Uribe Velez (elected in 2002)

National Anthem "Oh gloria inmarcesible! Oh júbilo inmortal!"; "Oh unfading glory! Oh immortal joy!" (written in 1905)

Important Holidays New Year's Day (January 1); Epiphany/Day of the Kings (January 5–6); Candlemas (February 2); Carnival (February); Easter (March/April); Corpus Christi (May/June); Saint Peter and Saint Paul's Day (June 29); Colombian Independence Day (July 20); Battle of Boyacá (August 7); All Saints' Day (November 1); Independence of Cartagena (November 11); Virgin of Chinquinquirá (December 8); and Christmas Celebrations (December 16–25)

Currency Colombian Peso (2,338 COP = U.S. $1 as of March 2005)

Opposite: **American tourists soak up the beauty of the Amazon River as they travel on a houseboat.**

Glossary

Spanish Vocabulary

ajiaco santafereño (ah-hee-AH-koh sahn-tah-fay-RAYN-yoh): a soup eaten by Colombians around Bogotá made from avocados, chicken, corn on the cob, and capers.

arepas (ah-RE-pahs): cornbread.

bambuco (bahm-BOO-koh): a musical style of the Andean region influenced by Spanish instrumentation.

Bogotazo (boh-goh-TAH-zoh): a period of violence in Bogotá following the assassination of the prominent and popular Liberal Jorge Eliécer Gaitán in 1948.

buñuelos (boon-yoo-AY-lohs): deep-fried dough and cheese balls.

cachacos (kah-CHAH-kohs): the Spanish name for residents of Bogotá.

chiva (CHEE-vah): old-fashioned bus made of wood that is still widely used in the countryside. The bus is unique because it has wooden benches instead of seats, and the body of the bus is painted with bright colors.

compadrazgo (kohm-pah-DRAHZ-goh): the Colombian social institution of godparenting.

compadres (kohm-PAH-drays): godparents.

conquistador (cohn-KEES-tah-dohr): a sixteenth-century Spanish conqueror of the Americas.

cumbia (COOM-bee-ah): one of the most popular musical rhythms and dances of the Caribbean coast.

empanadas (aym-pah-NAH-dahs): pastries stuffed with meat and vegetables, eaten as snacks.

guanabana (gwah-NAH-bah-nah): a type of fruit that is green on the outside and white on the inside.

La Violencia (lah vee-oh-LAYN-see-ah): the period of violent civil war (1948–1966) between Colombia's two main political parties.

locros de choclos (LOH-krohs day CHOH-klohs): a soup eaten by people in southern Colombia, which is made from corn and potatoes.

molas (MOH-lahs): decorated textiles made by Cuna Indians.

palenques (pah-LAYN-kays): communities established by black Colombians who had escaped slavery.

rondón (rohn-DOHN): a soup made from seafood, coconut milk, yucca, and plantains, which is a specialty of San Andrés and Providencia.

ruanas (roo-AH-nahs): woolen garments worn by Colombian men and women.

rumba (ROOM-bah): an impromptu private or public party that includes music and drinking.

telenovela (tay-lay-noh-VAY-lah): a television soap opera.

tigrillo (tee-GREE-yoh): a small wild cat.

torbellino (tor-bayl-YEE-noh): a type of indigenous Colombian music and dance, with Spanish influences on instrumentation.

English Vocabulary

Central America: the area of North America that connects Mexico with South America and consists of Belize, Costa Rica, El Salvador, Guatemala, Honduras, Nicaragua, and Panama.

concordat: an agreement between the pope and the government for the regulation of church matters, such as the rights and liberties of the church, the teaching of religion in schools, the appointment of bishops, and questions about marriage and divorces.

correspondent: a newspaper reporter who writes articles about or reports particular types of news from a foreign country.

criollos (CREE-oh-yohs): people of white and mestizo parentage — the majority of Colombia's population.

department: a state in Colombia.

fortifications: buildings or walls that are constructed to protect a place from attack.

guerillas: politically motivated soldiers who try to change the existing political order through armed struggle.

heyday: a period of time marked by great success or achievements.

indigenous peoples: groups of people who originated in the place where they currently live instead of coming from some other place.

Latin America: the countries of Central and South America, Mexico, and the West Indies.

llanos: also known as Los Llanos, the vast grassy lowlands between the Andes Mountains and the Orinoco River.

matador: the main performer in a bullfight; the bullfighter who kills the bull.

mestizos: people of Indian and white parentage.

missionary: a person sent by a church to convert others to that faith or to carry out humanitarian work.

mulattoes: people of white and black parentage.

New Granada: the Spanish-controlled territory of Ecuador, Venezuela, and Panama, which gained its independence in 1819.

patois: a language that develops from a mixture of two or more languages.

pelagic: birds or animals living at or near the ocean surface.

picadors: the matador's assistants on horseback who, in the early part of a bullfight, attack the bull with a lance.

pre-Columbian: the cultures present before the arrival of Christopher Columbus and the European settlers to the Americas.

rebellion: violent action by a group of people to overthrow the government of their country.

rituals: traditional or repeated ceremonies or practices.

shantytown: a group of crude huts that houses poor people, usually in or near a large city.

South America: the fourth-largest continent in the world, which includes the countries of Argentina, Bolivia, Brazil, Chile, Colombia, Ecuador, French Guiana, Guyana, Paraguay, Peru, Suriname, Uruguay, and Venezuela.

More Books to Read

Alta Colombia: The Splendor of the Mountains. Cristobal von Rothkirch, Juan Pablo Ruiz, and Carlos Mauricio Vega (St. Martin's Press)

Botero: New Works on Canvas. Fernando Botero (Rizzoli)

Colombia. Major World Nations series. Tricia Haynes (Chelsea House)

Colombia From the Air. Benjamin Villegas (St. Martin's Press)

Colombia: The Gateway to South America. Exploring Cultures of the World series. Lois Markham (Benchmark)

The Conquerors of the New Kingdom of Granada. Jose Ignacio Avellaneda Navas (University of New Mexico Press)

Cultures of the World: Colombia. Jill Dubois (Benchmark)

Gardens of Colombia. J. G. Cobo Borda (St. Martin's Press)

The Life of Colombia. Jeremy Horner (Villegas Editores)

Magic Eyes: Scenes from an Andean Childhood. Wendy Ewald (Bay Press)

The Monkey People: A Colombian Folktale. Eric Metaxas and Diana Bryan (Simon and Schuster)

The Taste of Colombia. Benjamin Villegas (St. Martin's Press)

Videos

Lonely Planet Travel Survival Kit: Colombia. (Lonely Planet: Hawthorn, Australia)

Music of Latin America. (Hollywood Select Videos)

New Horizons for Human Rights. (UN Productions)

Web Sites

lcweb2.loc.gov/frd/cs/cotoc.html

www.colombiaemb.org/opencms/opencms/colkids/

www.lonelyplanet.com/destinations/south_america/colombia/

Due to the dynamic nature of the Internet, some web sites stay current longer than others. To find additional web sites, use reliable search engines with one or more of the following keywords to help you locate information on Colombia. Keywords: *Bogotá, Símon Bolívar, Botero, Colombian coffee, Colombian history, La Corrida, Magdalena.*

Index